KIDS HAVE FEELINGS, TOO, SERIES

Someone Special Died

By Joan Singleton Prestine
Illustrations by Virginia Kylberg

Fearon Teacher Aids
A Paramount Communications Company

Editorial Director: Virginia L. Murphy

Editor: Lisa Schwimmer

Illustration: Virginia Kylberg

Design: Marek/Janci Design

Cover Illustration: Virginia Kylberg

Cover Design: Lucyna Green

© Fearon Teacher Aids

A Division of Frank Schaffer Publications, Inc.

23740 Hawthorne Boulevard

Torrance, CA 90505-5927

ISBN 0-86653-929-8

Printed in the United States of America

1.987654321

Someone I love very much just died. I wonder what it will be like without him.

3

We used to go for walks,
and swing,
and skip stones on the pond.
But now he isn't here.

We used to play catch,
put together puzzles,
and read books.
But now he isn't here.

I miss him.
I can't believe
I won't ever see
him again.
Sometimes I pretend
he's still alive.

If I had been there, I wouldn't have let him die. But Mom says I couldn't have done anything to help keep him alive.

Mom says everything dies. Flowers die. Dogs die. People die.

"What happened when he died?"

"His body stopped working."

"**W**here did his body go?"

"**H**is body is buried in the cemetery."

He shouldn't have left me.
I loved him. It's not fair.
Sometimes I feel so mad,
I want to yell,
or hit my pillow,
or slam the door.

Sometimes I feel so sad,
that nothing makes me happy.
I just want to cry and cry.

21

Sometimes I don't
want to play with anyone.
Not DeAnna. Not Chris.
Not even my dog Corky.
I just want to be alone.

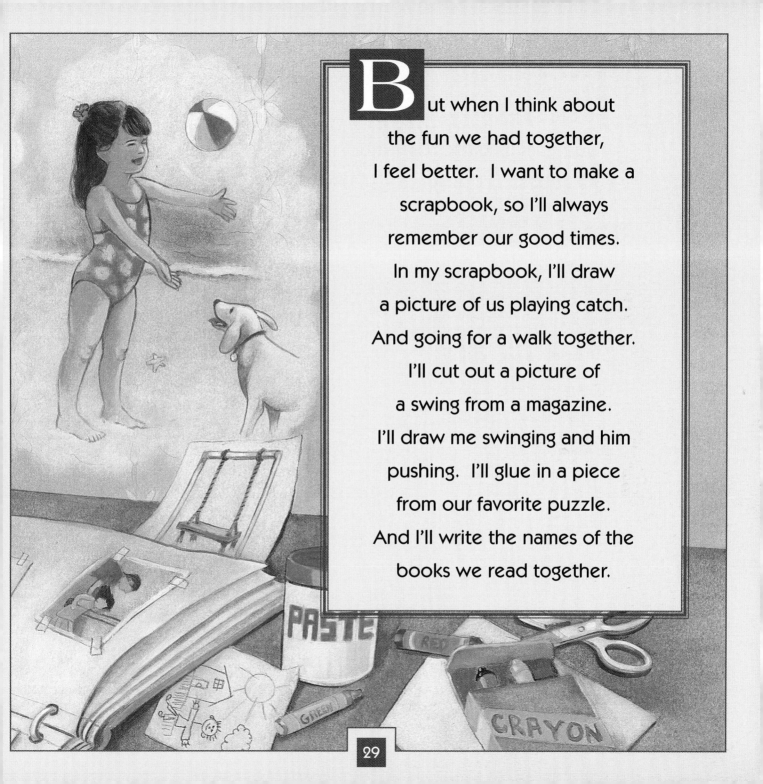

But when I think about
the fun we had together,
I feel better. I want to make a
scrapbook, so I'll always
remember our good times.
In my scrapbook, I'll draw
a picture of us playing catch.
And going for a walk together.
I'll cut out a picture of
a swing from a magazine.
I'll draw me swinging and him
pushing. I'll glue in a piece
from our favorite puzzle.
And I'll write the names of the
books we read together.

He died and I know he won't be coming back. But with my scrapbook, I'll never forget him.

iscussing *Someone Special Died* with Children

After reading the story, encourage discussion. Children learn from sharing their thoughts and feelings.

Discussion Questions for *Someone Special Died*

- What feelings did the little girl in the story have after the person she loved died?
- What did she remember doing with the person that she loved?
- How did she show she was sad?
- How did she show she was angry? Why do you think she was angry?
- Could she have saved the person she loved from dying? Why not?
- What did she do to help remember her happy feelings about the person that she loved?

Significance of *Someone Special Died* for Children

Sometimes a book will trigger strong feelings in young children, especially if they have experienced a similar situation. If they feel comfortable, encourage children to share their experiences.